PRUDENT PLANNING FOR FAMILY LEGACY

The Truth Behind Wills, Trusts, & Estates

SEDRIC E. COLLINS, ESQ.

Prudent [prood-nt][1]

adjective

Wise or judicious in practical affairs; careful in providing for the future.

---

[1] This definition was taken in part from dictionary.com

Jacobs & Whitehall
9600 Escarpment Blvd
Suite 745-282
Austin, TX 78749
(888) 570-7338
www.jacobsandwhitehall.com

Ordering Information:

Quantity sales. Special discounts are available on quantity purchases by corporations, associations, and others. For details, contact the publisher at the address above.

Orders by U.S. trade bookstores and wholesalers. Please contact Jacobs & Whitehall: Tel: (888) 570-7338 or visit www.jacobsandwhitehall.com.

Printed in the United States of America

Published in 2024

ISBN: 978-1-954506-77-0

FOREWORD

In my 25 years in the wealth management industry, I have found that when it comes to wills, trusts and estates, there are a lot of misconceptions out there. Regardless of success, education, and years in business, I often encounter folks who believe that a will is all that is needed to ensure everything goes smoothly and loved ones are taken care of at death. The following are just a few of the misconceptions that I consistently bump into as a financial professional:

- **Belief:** *A will allows you to decide when and how beneficiaries gain access to assets.*

Reality: Although a will can articulate who gets certain property, it cannot restrict or place conditions on how and when access is granted to property. On the contrary, trusts can set aside funds for the health, education, maintenance and support of beneficiaries and can restrict the sale of family assets such as businesses, real estate, art and other personal property.

- **Belief:** *Trusts and wills are both subject to Probate.*

  Reality: Generally, trusts are not subject to Probate, they may remain confidential, and they can be drafted in a manner that discourages others from contesting them in court. Conversely, wills *are* subject to Probate, open to the public, and can be contested in court. You often need a trust and a will as part of a comprehensive estate plan.

- **Belief:** *Trusts only start or take effect after you die.*

  Reality: Living trusts take effect during the lifetime of the creator of the trust and they assume possession and management of your liquid and illiquid assets.

- **Belief:** *All trusts, once established, can never be changed.*

  Reality: In most cases, a revocable living trust can be changed throughout the lifetime of the creator of the trust. However, irrevocable trusts cannot be changed or terminated, once created, without court intervention.

These misconceptions often leave families paralyzed by delaying the drafting and/or updating of estate plans. Our responsibility as trusted advisors is to walk clients through these important concepts and the associated risks of failing to put a plan in place. Unfortunately, I am no longer surprised by how hard some professionals and business owners work at their craft, yet they do not set aside time to "button up" what will happen to their legacy and assets beyond the grave.

It is great to partner with compassionate and knowledgeable estate planning professionals, such as Sedric Collins of Legacy One Law Firm, to navigate this confusing topic. From asking probing questions, which get to the heart of a family's legacy intentions; to drafting a roadmap to an optimized estate plan; my clients consistently rave about the relief they feel after working with the team at Legacy One Law Firm under Attorney Collins's leadership. This book is a roadmap designed to help families navigate the steps in the estate planning process more efficiently and to ensure the successful transfer of assets to the next generation.

– Stasia Washington, Managing Director & Senior Wealth Manager

Dedication

It may be inappropriate to write about family legacy without first acknowledging those in *my* family who have made it possible for me to share this message with you. First and foremost, I dedicate this book to my dear mother, Idella Yong, who with very limited education worked tirelessly to raise me and two of my younger siblings. Her love and devotion throughout the years is immeasurable. I'm eternally grateful to be her son and to have experienced so many life lessons under her care as a child.

Secondly, to my late grandfather, Eugene Collins, who was a decorated Army veteran, sage mentor, and community leader with a host of accolades that are forever forged with his legacy. His encouragement and support were instrumental in my decision to pursue a career as an attorney, and to become the man and father that I am today.

Finally, to every ancestor, educator, spiritual leader and friend who has provided a spark of inspiration or vote of confidence along this journey, this book is dedicated to each of you, collectively.

Disclaimer

This publication is intended to be used for educational purposes only. No legal advice is being given, and no attorney-client relationship is intended to be created by reading this material. The author assumes no liability for any errors or omissions or for how this book or its contents are used or interpreted, or for any consequences resulting directly or indirectly from the use of this book. For legal or any other advice, please consult an experienced attorney or the appropriate expert, who is aware of the specific facts of your case and is knowledgeable in the law in your jurisdiction.

LEGACY ONE LAW FIRM, APLC

1801 Century Park E, 24th Floor

Los Angeles, CA 90067

www.legacyonelaw.com

(323) 405-7017

TESTIMONIALS

"I originally met Sedric Collins through my networking group. My mother is 90 years old and has a trust that hadn't been reviewed or updated for many years. I invited Sedric to review my Mom's trust and he happily obliged. My sibling wanted to be present as well and Sedric made it very easy to coordinate with all of us and was flexible in his own schedule to make an in-home visit. I provided Sedric a copy of my Mom's trust in advance and when we met Sedric had a nice set of suggestions to update and improve the trust document. Sedric was professional and thorough as well as extremely accommodating. I highly recommend Sedric Collins and his firm, Legacy One Law Firm."

– Andrew Boron

****

"Sedric and team helped us secure our valuable assets and he really educated us. We are grateful."

– Tulani Watkins

****

"As an attorney, we are always skeptical of others performing legal work on our behalf. But Sedric was the absolute best!! Sedric set up my family's trust, will, and child care directives in a fast and efficient manner. Not only did he do great work, but he approached my family with a level of care and understanding in our estate planning needs. Sedric is the only attorney that I will trust with my family's future, and I hope you will give him a call so he can do the same for you!"

– Thomas Russell

****

"I highly recommend Sedric at Legacy One Law Firm for his trust and estate planning services. He was kind, caring, highly professional, and made the whole process easy. His price was very reasonable and affordable. I will value what he has created for me for the rest of my life, and so will my children. I am going to recommend his services to all of my family and friends."

– Christine McKenna

****

"Working with Sedric and Legacy One on our estate plan was beyond positive. Sedric was great at communicating with us and carefully explaining things throughout the planning process. He was also great at answering any questions we had. He really helped alleviate any concerns we had as well. We honestly can't recommend him enough."

– Mike Mcgrale

****

"Sedric was so great to work with. Extremely authentic and professional; took the time to understand my specific circumstances and provided his guidance; thoroughly explained complicated terms; very easy to talk to; understanding and patient; I immediately found myself trusting him. Overall, such a nice gentleman and great to work with. I now consider him my long-term life planner. I recommend him to anyone."

– Shanna Stout

****

"My team works with Sedric and Legacy One Law Firm to send our most trusted clients for estate planning. I can say that ALL of our clients that we have sent have had nothing but good things to say. Sedric's process is fair and thorough."

– Kelsey Wilson

****

"Sedric of Legacy One Law was absolutely AMAZING!!! He was very patient with my elderly parents. He took his time and went over the entire living trust process and answered all of their questions. He was fabulous!!!!"

– Timika Mason

****

"I was so grateful for Sedric and Legacy One Law Firm when I was creating my living trust for myself and my daughters. He was professional, ethical, knowledgeable, thorough and remains a trusted counsel to me. I highly recommend Legacy One Law Firm to protect your estate and heirs."

– Selina Thomas

****

TABLE OF CONTENTS

About The Author

My very first job after passing the California bar exam was as in-house legal counsel for a small university located in the San Fernando Valley of California. Unfortunately, after about 50 years of being in business, that school had to close its doors. This put me in the precarious position of deciding what direction I wanted to go rather early in my career. There were three paths set before me: venture into corporate America, pursue a job at a law firm, or "hang my own shingle" by opening my own law firm.

Around the same time period, I was saddened by the deaths of several prominent entertainers whose music had impacted the lives of millions. They shall remain nameless for the scope of this writing, but you'd be hard-pressed to find someone in the western hemisphere who had not heard at least one of their hits on television or radio. Personally, one of the things that I found most disturbing about their passing was that these iconic celebrities did not have their financial affairs in order. More specifically, they each died without having a will or a living trust, and as a result, their loved ones endured the unpleasant reality of probate court and extended periods of conflict. After learning the fates of at least three of these entertainers, I was compelled to figure out what it was about estate planning that might discourage people with significant, or fairly modest, financial resources from getting a plan in writing. With that goal in mind, and after hours of research, I learned that a whopping 60% of Americans do not have any form of estate planning in place - not even a simple will. I found these numbers to be staggering and simply unacceptable given their importance in the grand scheme of things.

As it pertained to my family members, circle of friends, and colleagues, the numbers didn't fare much better. In fact, it has become much too common to see fundraisers on social media pages and other reactive approaches to dealing with the death or incapacity of a loved one. Clearly, the need to have uncomfortable conversations with families was apparent, and the need to put their wishes in writing was long overdue. However, to borrow from a biblical text, *the harvest is ripe, but the laborers few.* Simply put, a career as an trusts and estates attorney was certainly not the popular choice among my peers in law school nor is it glorified by actors on television. I can recall thinking to myself, no one actually goes to law school to draft wills and trusts, right? Nevertheless, there was a silver lining to being laid off so early in my legal career, and moreover, a greater opportunity to be of service to the community at large. It was in this manner that estate planning found me, and soon thereafter, the vision of Legacy One Law Firm was born.

In the early days of my law practice, I served mostly friends, family members, and colleagues who were gracious enough (or brave enough) to entrust me with their family legacy. Don't worry, those early clients turned out just fine. In fact, those early clients began to share their planning experiences with other family members, co-workers, and friends. Word traveled fast, and today, we serve clients across the entire state of California. From young professionals, to seasoned business owners, to retired empty nesters, our clients come from all walks of life.

Given the diversity of ages, life stages, and financial circumstances of our clients, we have seen a myriad of problems and pitfalls that come from improper estate planning. From this, we have developed a holistic approach that takes into account not only an individual's short-term goals, but their intermediate and long-term goals as well. We don't focus on merely planning for death. Rather, our services emphasize planning for life. Isn't that what we all want? More life, or at minimum a better life for those we will one day leave behind.

What's more, our experience has shown us firsthand that estate planning doesn't work with a one-size-fits-all, cookie-cutter approach. As such, we look at a wide range of contingencies, such as children getting older, or the possibility of a client becoming incapacitated. We take into account unique family dynamics, which may include whether or not siblings get along, blended family concerns, and any other nuances to your family that make this planning so much more of a personalized journey.

Our team, at Legacy One, doesn't focus solely on the transactional document preparation that is commonly found at traditional law firms. We provide a customized, holistic approach to planning while ensuring that the individual's needs and desires, as well as their unique personal and family values, are taken into account.

The Goal Of This Book

Our goal here is simple: to educate and empower *you* to make informed decisions regarding the actions required to ensure that the things that *you* have, and the people or organizations that *you* care about, are taken care of in the manner in which *you* decide.

If you care about what happens to the people that you love and the things that you've worked hard to build, this book is for you. If you want to protect those assets you've accumulated over a lifetime, but feel overwhelmed about getting started, this book is for you. If you've been putting off planning for your family legacy by procrastinating and "kicking the can down the road," this book is for you.

We understand how easy it is to put off estate planning, especially when it may seem complicated and overwhelming. Unfortunately, many people put off planning for too long and become incapacitated or pass away before they ever get around to it. It's our goal to remove uncertainty from the process and give you a firm foundation on which you can begin to take control of your future, and secure your family, individual, or business legacy. It is my desire to lay the foundation for accomplishing all of the above.

CHAPTER 1

COMMON MISCONCEPTIONS ABOUT ESTATE PLANNING

A great place to start is where many people get it wrong. We call these "the planning pitfalls" or simply put, the things that either hold folks back from planning or leave families with unexpected legal fees after insufficient planning. The most common myths and misconceptions about estate planning that I have encountered over the years are as follows:

1. **Financial limitations**—One does not have enough assets or financial resources to begin estate planning.
2. **Time is on my side**—One is too young or healthy to begin estate planning.
3. **Everything will turn out fine**—My spouse and kids will automatically get everything I own.
4. **"One-and-done" planning**—One only needs to execute a will or trust once, and it is good for a lifetime.

Financial limitations

Estate: (noun) e.state - all the money and property owned by a particular person, especially at death.

– Oxford Languages Dictionary

One of the most common phrases I've heard over the years when discussing preparing a will or trust with potential clients, friends, and strangers is "I don't really own any property or assets right now, but when I do…" The truth is that once you start planning, you realize that you have a lot more than you thought. Maybe you have a couple of life insurance policies, a 401K, and own a home – but you've never really considered what those assets are really worth. For instance, it's incredibly common for homeowners in California to think that they don't have much when, in reality, they may have an estate worth a couple of million dollars when factoring in the real estate, retirement accounts, and life insurance policies of two adults in a household.

Perhaps the most overlooked asset in one's financial portfolio is life insurance. For those who are unfamiliar, a life insurance policy pays out a lump sum monetary amount at the death of the person who is insured. It's generally referred to as the "death benefit" within an insurance policy. For most adults in reasonably good health, a life insurance policy with a $250-500,000 death benefit is affordable and may be easily obtained (consult with a licensed life insurance agent for your specific case). In fact, the cost of a term life insurance policy that could leave hundreds of thousands of dollars to your desired beneficiary(ies) may cost significantly less than some of the leisurely activities and non-essential items that are purchased each month. What might you be willing to sacrifice to ensure your loved ones are cared for in your absence?

For those who presently have life insurance, how would it feel to know that the death benefit or payout from that policy would be used in the manner in which you decide and not squandered or mismanaged by a beneficiary?

For those who do not have life insurance, how would it feel to have an asset that could make life a little easier financially for those you leave behind?

Therefore, do not let the belief that you do not have enough create a barrier between you and the peace of mind that comes from knowing you've established a written plan to benefit those whom you love. The little that you do have could mean a lot to someone else when there's a plan in place for how the money will be spent.

Time is on my side

When it comes to our mortality, most are familiar with the cliché phrases, "Tomorrow is not promised…" or "We don't know which day will be our last." Unfortunately, in my line of work, I either directly or indirectly deal with the reality of those statements. I am reminded of a potential client who contacted our firm after reading one of our blog articles online. We'll call her Jill, for the sake of this story. Jill had always wanted to put a plan in place, but due to the state of her health at the time (which was in decline), she felt the time was right to take action. Jill was in her fifties, but had understood the importance of estate planning for several years. She contacted our firm for a free consultation, scheduled a planning session, and received our client questionnaire in the mail. However, on the day of her scheduled planning session, we reached out to Jill several times by phone and email with no success. We initially thought that she'd simply forgotten or another more important matter arose. Nevertheless, roughly seven days later we received a phone call from her brother who had found our questionnaire on the kitchen table in Jill's home. He wanted to know if we were the law firm that prepared Jill's Last Will and Testament. He'd searched the house thoroughly, but could not find it. He'd only found the questionnaire that we'd mailed to her regarding plans to discuss her final wishes. We were saddened to learn that Jill had passed away several days before her scheduled planning session. No will was ever prepared - and her reason for not showing up was not due to procrastination or forgetfulness, it was that she'd died before completing the process.

One may think that time is at their disposal because of youth, good health, or perhaps good fortune, but the reality is that none of us know how much time we have left on this earth or if our health may be suddenly compromised. Our firm has helped clients in their mid-twenties with foundational estate planning, despite just beginning their careers and with few assets accumulated. Estate planning helps us prepare both for anticipated life events *and* the unforeseen tragedies that no one expects to encounter.

Everything will turn out fine

"Everything will turn out fine" is what he assured his wife as he declined what would be her final request to create a living trust that would benefit their children. George was a blue-collar small business owner from San Diego who, at the time, was in his second marriage having children from each. He firmly believed that the law would divide everything equally between his wife and children in the event of his demise, and therefore, to hire someone to put this in writing was purely a waste of time. Well, George was not completely wrong in his assertions. The law does have a set of default rules or laws in place for those who do not express their wishes via a will or living trust. However, George's plan to *not* have a plan would be accompanied by a few unforeseen wrinkles that did not bode well for those he left behind.

To summarize, George had been married twice and had children from both marriages. Unfortunately, his relationship with the adult children from his first marriage was strained and tense after a bitter divorce from their mother. He'd spoken to them very sparingly over the course of a decade. Hence, there was no discussion or written instructions as to what constituted a fair distribution of property among his surviving children and his soon-to-be widow. After George's sudden and unexpected death, his estranged children appeared at his widow's home requesting to see copies of any will or trust that their late father had prepared. George's widow was caught off guard by these events, and she'd already lost a significant amount of sleep from grieving the loss of her husband. She was forced to "lawyer up" and hire someone to represent her interests in probate court.

Furthermore, George had business and personal property that was in his name alone. Thankfully, the house that they'd purchased during their marriage would be free from any claims… so she (the widow) thought. However, his widow would later learn that George's half of the house was subject to the claims of his estranged children and other creditors as part of the probate process.

Ultimately, George was not wrong, the law did make a division of his assets between his surviving spouse and children, however, not before a two-year grueling court battle involving his estranged children who believed that his widow was the only thing standing in the way of what was rightfully theirs by inheritance.

Please note that this type of post-death dispute is not limited to those having blended families and multiple marriages. Sibling feuds and conflicts account for a significant amount of post-death disputes both in and out of court and often involve traditional and blended family members. No family is "immune" to conflict, even with proper planning and great intentions. Imagine how frustrating it might be for those without anything in place at all.

"One-and-done" planning

Finally, we are not here to spotlight only the misconceptions and myths held by those who fail to plan. There is an erroneous line of thinking held by some who do have an estate plan in place. I like to refer to this myth as the "one-and-done" transactional approach to legacy and estate planning. Here, once an estate plan is established, it is never revisited until someone has died or become incapacitated, which is often too late to make favorable changes for beneficiaries. For example, we often conduct comprehensive reviews of estate plans that were prepared by other law firms. Some of these plans are 20-25 years old and have yet to be updated. Prior to opening my law practice, while still employed as legal counsel for the university, I was approached by a professor who had heard of my plans to serve the community by way of estate planning. She shared with me, embarrassingly, that she and her spouse established a trust when their daughter was seven years old. Her daughter at the time of this conversation was in her late twenties. They'd never reviewed their plan again nor had they been in contact with the attorney that prepared it. Her sage advice to me was, "Find a way to keep in contact with your clients over the years." At the time of this conversation, I was not fully aware of how important this advice from a non-attorney was.

As time went by, and more reviews were conducted, I discovered that one of the primary ways that estate plans fail is that they simply become outdated. Over time, so many aspects of our lives are subject to change. The laws change, beneficiaries change, assets change, and oftentimes our personal wishes change. Is it not appropriate that our living trusts and other essential documents accurately reflect these changes?

We will end this chapter with this thought: Will the plan that you currently have in place work the way that you intend for it to work when the time comes?

CHAPTER 2

THE IMPORTANCE OF ESTATE PLANNING

Estate planning isn't simply planning or preparing for death, it's planning for life. This approach can be viewed in a couple of different ways: First, a living trust with disability provisions can address instances where you or your significant other have become incapacitated. For instance, if you are severely injured in an accident or become mentally incapacitated due to age or illness. If this were to occur, who will manage your finances, control your assets, or make critical healthcare decisions on your behalf during your lifetime? Secondly, consider the afterlife, but not in the way it is commonly thought of. I'm referring to notion that there will likely be life *after* your life when you consider loved ones who are left behind. The plan that you put in place today may enrich their lives for years to come, when set up properly. In fact, history has shown that with the right legal guidance and a properly executed estate plan, both families and single adults can…

- Make informed and empowered decisions,
- Ensure assets aren't lost to the state or federal government upon death,
- Protect assets from creditors, predators, bankruptcies, and divorce,
- Keep family members out of court and out of conflict upon incapacity or death,
- Obtain access to a lifetime of legal and financial guidance through a relationship with a trusted advisor.

In the paragraphs to follow, we'll pull back the curtain and reveal what typically happens in the absence of a legally enforceable plan. Additionally, we'll further illustrate the importance of estate planning and why it's one of the greatest gifts you can give to yourself and to your family.

Dying Without Having Any Planning In Place

In most states, dying without a will is called 'intestacy', or to die intestate. If you don't have a written and legally valid plan in place at the time of your death, the state of California (and most other states in America) will have a plan for you. Unfortunately, you and the ones you leave behind are unlikely to appreciate how the state's plan will unfold in the aftermath.

Here is a brief explanation: Each state has default rules or laws in place for those who pass away without a valid will or a living trust. These rules are carried out and enforced in a court process known as probate. In short, the probate process is basically litigation that is opened up against your estate at death, using your own assets, and is for the benefit of your creditors first. Whatever is left after the creditors get their share of your property will then go to your heirs, who (from a legal standpoint) are the surviving next of kin in the order of priority that is predetermined by the government.

In California, probate can be a stressful six to twenty-four-month process and may cost your family tens of thousands of dollars, therefore drastically reducing the inheritance left to spouses, children, and grandchildren. In many cases, we have seen estate and probate bills exceeding six figures. To be clear, when you don't have your affairs in order, the state has an immediate financial interest in the property you leave behind whether you voluntarily or involuntarily use its process. Sounds fair? Well, it's the law. Moreover, the state is not doing your family any favors by wrapping up your affairs. Probate is a big business for the state and the lawyers who represent families that are at the mercy of this default system. Unfortunately, this process is inevitable for the heirs of those dying with a fair amount of property and without the right plan in place.

Dying With Only A Will

There is an old saying in my line of work: "Where there's a will, there's a probate."

Even if you have a will in place at death, no matter how well it is written, you are voluntarily signing your loved ones up for the undesirable probate process because (in most states) a judge will determine whether your will is valid and enforceable under law. However, if you pass away with very modest means, let's say total assets valued below $50,000.00, probate may be avoided and the court may require only legal documents to be completed before access to the bank accounts, vehicles, or other personal property of the deceased person can be legally granted. In other words, the poorer you are the easier the process. Thus, one solution or "plan" is to simply die broke, not leaving one red cent for anyone to squabble over. There will be no lawyers, no court, or paperwork to deal with. Undoubtedly, this might work for a few, but for most of us, a plan with more substance is needed to provide for those whom we love.

Speaking of those whom we love, from a practical standpoint, someone you love - be it a surviving spouse or child - is going to have to hire legal representation in the wake of your passing. They must find someone to represent your estate and navigate the complex business of death once the initial grieving has subsided. At that point, legal questions and/or issues will certainly arise. There will be a determination of whether there is a will or trust in place. If there is a valid will in place, then the executor, who is the person that you've appointed to manage your final affairs, must now execute your final wishes, but not without the supervision of a lawyer and the probate court. Furthermore, whether or not someone becomes an executor depends on several factors that the court will consider. For example, the court may look at the character, creditworthiness, and whether the person selected is able to be bonded. Therefore, the favorite nephew or the responsible child who was appointed in your will may or may not be the person the court deems qualified to serve as executor of your estate. Yes, the court has more hurdles, even for those who are fairly prepared.

As it pertains to the role of the executor, this person shall represent the entire estate and serve as a liaison between the court and the rest of the family. They may be asked to assist with gathering assets and making distributions to beneficiaries under the guidance of a lawyer. The executor must be trustworthy and should be somewhat knowledgeable about the family and financial affairs of the decedent (the person who has died). With that said, we believe that you, and not the court, are in the best position to appoint an executor to interact with your family. Consider this: for those who do not have a will in place, the court will appoint an executor, who may be a complete stranger, to take an inventory of personal property and handle other matters, which may be considered intrusive to the surviving members of the family. Is family privacy something that you value?

Once the lawyer has been hired and the executor is in place, probate proceedings may begin. This often means that someone in your family, if appointed executor, may have to take time away from work to attend meetings and court hearings, inventory assets, manage family disputes, and deal with any other matter pertaining to wrapping up your final affairs with the court. This may be bearable for a short period of time, but in states like California, probate can last a couple of years or more. This begs the question: Is all of this time, energy, and effort necessary to distribute the property of someone who supposedly did the *right* thing by preparing a will? Then there is the question of whether creating a simple will is ever the right thing to do for those looking to avoid court and conflict.

What If There Are Minor Children Involved?

If you've passed away without a plan, and there is no surviving parent who is willing or able to raise your minor children living at home, the court will oversee a guardianship process to appoint a new parent/legal guardian to step into your shoes. As a parent, I understand what it's like to lay awake at night wondering what would happen to my child should anything ever happen to me. If you've experienced the same or similar thoughts, then you may agree that the idea of your child being in the custody or care of strangers is very unsettling. Regardless of whether that is a concern for you or not, you'd likely agree that the court is not in the best position to determine who should raise a child.

Without an estate plan, which includes the proper nomination documents signed by a parent, the court must determine the most suitable guardian for a child from among the relatives or friends that petition the court for guardianship. The challenge here is the court doesn't know the personalities, values, strengths, and weaknesses of these individuals like the parent(s) would have known. How detrimental would it be to an orphaned child to be left in the care of an unfit parent? The process of nominating both temporary and long-term guardians is often overlooked without proper legal guidance, and the court is left with the critical task of determining who will raise a child in the absence of input from the deceased parents. Also, be sure to read Chapter 4 for other considerations regarding estate planning with minor children still living at home.

As you can see, there is a lot that takes place "behind the curtain" when someone passes away without a proper plan in place. Even those with a simple will may be exposing loved ones to a bevy of court proceedings and unintended legal expenses. This is merely the tip of the iceberg. When adding family disputes over property to the mix, the stress and the price tag for wrapping up an estate only compounds.

Don't Wait To Start Planning

As mentioned earlier, it is well-documented that nearly 60% of Americans do not have an estate plan in place. Most people know that they need to take care of this, but life gets in the way and it distracts many from getting started. You may be telling yourself that you will get around to it after buying that house, once you've saved up a little more for retirement, or once the kids have gone off to college.

Life is unpredictable. We don't know when our time will be up. All this sounds cliché, however, this is one of the few areas in life where we know the cliché applies to all of us. Thus, there's no better time than the present because the present is really all we have. The longer we wait, the higher the probability that we will become part of the 60% of non-planners who put their loved ones through probate each year. When we think of it from that perspective, it will create a higher sense of urgency to take action. The alternative is to take the reactionary approach of waiting for life to hit us where it hurts in the form of critical illness, incapacity, or sudden death.

It's Never Too Early To Start Planning

If you are an adult reading this passage of text, then this applies to you: If or when your health deteriorates to the point where you no longer understand the basic elements of your estate, either due to dementia, Alzheimer's, or another debilitating incapacitation, you will be unable to plan for your estate. You will have lost knowledge of who your family members are, forgotten what your assets are, or have lost the ability to comprehend the process of estate planning in general. At this point, the law has determined that you no longer have the capacity to prepare a will or establish a trust.

Short of that, however, it is never too early or too late to begin the estate planning process. We encourage you to take a proactive response to planning while you still have your full capacities as opposed to a reactionary response, as mentioned above. At that point, it becomes either too late or vastly more expensive due to court involvement.

Take it from a trusted advisor who is a participant in this process, whenever you involve the court system, the price tag for a solution increases exponentially. For those who are waiting until they have more, you may never get to more. Start a plan with what you have today and revise or amend that plan in the future, if and when the time comes.

Estate Planning During College

If you're at least 18 years old and you have any property that you care about, you may be best served by having at least a basic plan. We will discuss what that entails below. Once you're 18 years old, your parents have lost the legal authority to govern what happens in your life. You're now an adult. As mentioned previously, an estate plan is not limited to what happens when you die, but it also addresses what happens when you're incapacitated. And despite the fact that you may *feel* invincible at this age, the reality is you're a vulnerable member of humanity that must plan for life's unexpected setbacks.

If you're the parent of a college-aged child, your children should have an advanced healthcare directive and durable financial power of attorney documents in place at a minimum. In the absence of such, you will be prohibited from making critical financial and healthcare decisions on their behalf, should they become incapacitated. Only weeks prior to finalizing this book, we received a call from a client who received chilling news that her daughter, who was attending college out of state, had to undergo emergency surgery for an infection that had spread to her soft tissue. With less than 24 hours of notice, we were able to get the incapacity documents needed to ensure that our client would be able to access her daughter's medical records and make healthcare decisions during this time of vulnerability.

In short, if you're old enough to legally sign a contract, you're old enough to sign a living trust and create a will with instructions for the distribution of your personal property. Moreover, you're old enough to create healthcare documents and powers of attorney that will save your family the financial and emotional stress that comes from petitioning the court for permission under dire circumstances.

CHAPTER 3

ESSENTIAL DOCUMENTS FOR A COMPREHENSIVE ESTATE PLAN

All too often, we see what we like to call "piecemeal estate planning." This term is applicable when we encounter someone having only a will and nothing else, or perhaps a trust and nothing else. They may have a healthcare directive in place, but only because they had an impending surgery and their primary healthcare provider requested that it be done. Although these documents are components of a comprehensive estate plan, as standalone legal documents, they leave an individual or family vulnerable to a myriad of legal issues when tragedy strikes.

Your comprehensive estate plan should include these essential documents:

- Testamentary will or revocable living trust
- A pour-over will (if using a revocable living trust)
- The appropriate healthcare directive that applies in your state,
- A durable financial power of attorney,
- Guardianship nominations (Discussed in Chapter 4), and
- Final disposition instructions (to detail whether you want to be buried, cremated, etc.).

Testamentary Will

A will is a testamentary document expressing the final wishes of a person and it only "speaks" at the death of the *testator,* which is the individual whose wishes are expressed in the document. Since time immemorial, there have been wills. The use of wills as a means of transferring ownership of property at death dates back to ancient Greek and Roman history. Although they were not called "wills" in their early adoption into society, many of the same formalities surrounding their creation, such as the presence of witnesses during the signing, still hold true today. Moreover, due to their long-standing tradition and widespread use, wills are arguably the most popular legal document for end-of-life preparations, as they are often discussed in the media and featured in films.

Perhaps the most ideal scenario that many envision for preparing a will is one where death does not occur until a ripe old age and family members are present at bedside. Finally, just before taking a final breath, the "Last Will and Testament" is signed before drifting off into the afterlife. This sounds much like the final scene of a movie, right? We inherently understand that the end may not turn out that way for many of us, so we must deal with the reality of our mortality in a way that is practical, and in a manner that ensures the people we care about and the things we care about are taken care of. Certainly, preparing a will is a great place to start. However, relying on a will as the primary document in your estate planning portfolio has several limitations that we discuss below.

First and foremost, a will only speaks at death. As discussed earlier in the book, the mindset that we hope that you'll adopt is that estate planning is planning for life. A will does not address the possibility of incapacitation or the disability of the testator because the will doesn't become valid or legally enforceable until the testator's death. Therefore, it's very short-sighted with regard to life's unpredictable circumstances, and may expose one's family to increased legal expenses and stress in the aftermath of a sharp decline in health.

Secondly, a will's primary function is limited to the distribution of property at death. Under the court's supervision, assets will be distributed to known or discoverable heirs, which presents a separate set of issues for those with little-to-no family remaining at death. A gift left via a will is often called a "bequest" or a "devise". Here, one is articulating wishes to transfer property to a named individual, class of individuals, or a charitable organization. Commonly, these gifts are left to family members or next of kin, many of whom are under the age of eighteen or unprepared to manage the property to be inherited.

What is unbeknownst to the well-intentioned testator of the will, is the court merely has the power to distribute wealth, not to supervise the preservation of it. In fact, even the most competent of probate courts will not have the personnel or resources to oversee what happens to property and financial resources once it has been transferred to the heir. Thus, planning with a will doesn't allow for the long-term planning that one may have in mind for children or grandchildren.

As it pertains to the squandering or mismanagement of the property that you leave behind, if your child or named beneficiary in your will is only 18 years old at the time you pass away, and they've inherited a generous one million dollar estate, do you believe that they will possess the financial literacy or maturity to make wise decisions with such an inheritance? Consider what you might have done with even half the size of that inheritance at the tender age of 18. How many extravagant vacations, fancy dinners, and expensive cars would it have taken to deplete that inheritance? Unfortunately, we've seen dreams of passing down generational wealth come to a screeching halt when said wealth is distributed outright through a will. The lack of long-term planning and wealth preservation is perhaps the most glaring limitation of a testamentary will.

To summarize, a will only plans for events after death and does not take into account the long-term preservation of what is left behind. For those of us who'd like to keep real estate in the family, plan for college education, ensure children are provided for over an extended period of time, and place conditions on gifts that align with our values, a will falls short as the primary instrument in an estate plan. Nevertheless, for those with very modest means, no real estate or other significant assets, a testamentary will may be sufficient. A conversation with a qualified legal professional that focuses on estate planning will help in determining whether planning with a will is in your best interest.

Trusts

In its simplest form, a trust is nothing more than a contract that allows you to govern the relationship that you have with your property as it relates to your beneficiaries. It allows for the greatest degree of control as to who will receive property, when they receive it, and the conditions that may either qualify or disqualify a beneficiary from receiving the property. I like to jokingly say to clients that planning with a trust is the closest thing to speaking from the grave that we'll encounter. When set up properly, a living trust with the appropriate disability provisions is the best way to manage and preserve assets over multiple generations, if desired.

Generally, a trust can be *irrevocable,* which means it cannot be changed, amended, or terminated after its creation; or *revocable,* which means it can be amended, or dissolved by the creators of the trust for any reason. For the purposes of this book and for estate planning, we will focus on the *revocable* living trust because of the flexibility that it offers to the creator. So why is it called a "living trust"? A living trust is a financial instrument that takes effect during the settlor's lifetime, as opposed to a testamentary trust, which takes effect at death. The "settlor" or "trustor" is the person or people who have created the trust.

As mentioned above, as the settlor of a living trust, you can decide how and when the things that you've worked hard for are distributed. You are also able to place certain contingencies on those gifts. For example, if my child attends and completes college, they shall be entitled to a monetary gift of $200,000.00 upon graduation. There are countless other conditions and contingencies that can be included in a trust. Suppose a beneficiary becomes critically ill, has a drug addiction, or becomes disabled. A well-drafted trust can speak to those life events by making financial provisions to support the beneficiary according to the circumstances that have arisen. As such, a living trust is arguably the most prudent choice for establishing and efficiently passing down generational wealth. Don't take my word for it. Consider the iconic Rockefellers and the Carnegies who used trusts as the cornerstone for the transfer and management of their wealth, which endured for generations.

Conversely, it cannot be all sunshine and roses when planning with a living trust. While there are many benefits to having a trust, there are also some limitations. One limitation of a trust is that a trust is only as good as the language that supports and upholds it. Specifically, the language that is actually drafted in the trust. This is why proper trust planning under the guidance of a qualified legal professional is essential. As the saying goes, "You don't know what you don't know." So, consequently, you (as an inexperienced drafter) will not likely know what essential language is missing from your trust.

There is also a duration on how long a trust can last. In California, this duration is about 90 years or no later than 21 years after the death of an individual who was alive at the time that trust was established. What's more, the trust could be subject to abuse without the right successor trustees and advisors in place to help maintain the trust over the years. If one does not appoint a competent or financially responsible individual or company to manage the assets and carry out the instructions of the trust, problems may arise. Thus, sound advice on who should serve in a key role, such as successor trustee, should be sought before the trust is established.

Finally, a trust does not guarantee that your children will not fight over assets after your passing, however, it can greatly minimize and discourage disputes. Whether or not your children will fight over your assets is heavily dependent on the personalities of your children. Presumably, you know your children better than anyone else. If they don't get along while you're alive, the likelihood that they'll get along when there's a house, money, and other assets at stake is probably not high. In fact, independent studies on family dynamics after the death of a parent have shown that nearly 44% of post-death disputes involve sibling rivalries.

Let's be clear, your trust is not going to prevent your children from arguing, but having clear, written instructions on what happens to certain assets will help mitigate or significantly reduce the probability that disputes will occur. In fact, a skillfully drafted trust will include "No-Contest" provisions and other language that will discourage beneficiaries from bringing frivolous or meritless claims in court regarding the distribution plan outlined in your trust.

The Misconceptions

The Foreword in this book outlined some of the misconceptions regarding estate planning with trusts. From my experience, some common misconceptions about planning with a trust include the belief that one loses the ability to sell, gift, or dispose of assets placed in a trust. This is not true. A revocable living trust allows the settlor to maintain and dispose of property in the same manner as before the trust was created. Others have the misconception that creating a revocable living trust will negatively impact your personal taxes and finances. In truth, however, a revocable trust as used for estate planning purposes is not going to create additional tax liability because the settlor merely funds the trust with property that they already owned and maintained prior to the creation of the trust. Although, they may still add assets to the trust moving forward. The Internal Revenue Service (IRS) code has provisions designed to facilitate favorable tax outcomes for those who wish to prudently plan for their estates. Be sure to consult with your tax professional or attorney to learn more about how these laws work in greater detail.

Different Types Of Trusts

There are a myriad of different types of trusts, which are created for various purposes. However, for estate planning, we can narrow the scope down to a few: the disclaimer trust, the intentionally defective marital deduction trust, the Clayton election trust, and the probate avoidance trust. Speaking to an experienced estate planning lawyer to explore which trust is right for you is strongly recommended before establishing one for your household. We will briefly discuss these few below.

Disclaimer Trust

The most common trust that we see is the disclaimer trust. This trust gives the surviving spouse the ability to disclaim a portion of the deceased spouse's estate for estate tax planning purposes. In many cases, it is an "all to the survivor" trust, which transfers the bulk of the deceased spouse's estate to the surviving spouse.

For example, if the family's assets exceed the federal estate tax threshold, a disclaimer trust may help mitigate the tax liability owed to the federal government. In short, a portion of the deceased spouse's estate may be disclaimed by the surviving spouse, thereby reducing the size of the taxable estate. This works by placing the disclaimed assets into a separate trust whereby the surviving spouse may receive the income generated by a secondary or marital deduction trust.

Utilizing a disclaimer trust may serve two purposes: First, it allows the surviving spouse to defer estate taxes to the second death (the death of the surviving spouse). Second, it allows the surviving spouse to reduce the size of the taxable estate while still allowing them to enjoy the benefits of the deceased spouse's assets through the secondary trust that is created.

Intentionally Defective Marital Deduction Trust

The intentionally defective marital deduction trust is a trust for families that have concerns about whether or not a spouse will remarry and possibly disinherit children either intentionally or by mistake. As a part of our interview process, when we're getting to know a family, we will ask about the fears or concerns regarding what happens if one spouse should pass away first.

As alluded to above, a common concern of a parent might be that they don't want the children of their marriage to be potentially disinherited by virtue of an estate plan drafted with a future spouse after they have died. Let's face it, life goes on after we pass away, and if a surviving spouse shall venture to marry again, someone else's rights and wishes may come into play.

Moreover, another concern might be that one spouse does not desire for a future spouse to receive a share of the assets they've worked hard to build during the current marriage. For clients with concerns of this nature, the intentionally defective marital deduction trust may include certain provisions and safeguards designed to protect those interests and alleviate some of these concerns.

Clayton Election Trust

The Clayton election trust is perfect for our blended families. In California, the divorce rate is rather high. This trust design allows for a trust to automatically split into two trusts at the death of the first spouse. Here, there is either an automatic creation of a separate trust or the duty of the trustee to establish a separate trust for the benefit of separate children, a separate organization or both. Typically, we see the Clayton Election utilized when there are kids from prior marriages or relationships and it makes sense to make separate provisions.

Probate Avoidance Trust

The probate avoidance trust is just as it sounds, a trust that is established to keep the assets of the settlor out of probate. This is a great option for singles, single parents, business owners, and anyone who desires to keep their family out of court and conflict. It should be noted that all trusts will avoid probate if set up properly. With that said, there are several factors that would determine whether or not your trust will end up in probate. The most common that we encounter is whether or not a trust has been properly funded. Funding a trust means that a trust either owns assets by having the assets titled in the name of the living trust or, alternatively, the trust controls the asset because it has been properly named as the primary or contingent beneficiary of the asset.

Failure to fund the trust is one of the most common missteps with living trusts. Simply put, if you fail to properly fund the trust, then the assets that you intend to pass to beneficiaries will remain subject to probate because the assets are still in your legal name as opposed to the name of the trust. The same holds true for real estate, investment accounts, bank accounts, life insurance policies with minor children as beneficiaries, and any other asset that is in your name when you pass away. It's essential that you seek the guidance of a qualified attorney for advice on how this process works and which method is appropriate for your individual situation.

Healthcare Documents In Estate Planning

In California, we advise that all adults over the age of 18 have a California advanced healthcare directive (as long as they have the ability and mental capacity to do so). If one has a disability that precludes them from having the ability to enter a contract, or make financial decisions independently, that person would not likely be able to create a California advanced healthcare directive.

A California advanced healthcare directive allows you to appoint someone who you trust to make medical decisions and end-of-life decisions on your behalf when you no longer have the ability to do so.

Most of us have heard of living wills and "do not resuscitate" clauses, yet many of us have not taken steps to put these wishes in writing in our own lives. Unfortunately, there have been significant legal battles over whether or not someone should be kept on life support or whether someone should be fed through a feeding tube. The outcome is often family conflict and financial hardship. How much easier would things be if the wishes of the person enduring this health crisis were written and made available to health care providers and decision makers within the family unit?

As it pertains to you, the reader, what happens if you have an allergic reaction to certain medications or if you have been prescribed medication for a health condition? If you do not have the ability to communicate these things, who will have that knowledge upon your incapacity? In an emergency or life-threatening situation, you may not have access to your primary care provider and others may need critical information at a moment's notice.

An emergency crew or "first responders" will not likely know that you're allergic to penicillin or any other medication. They won't know whether the medications that you're currently taking will have adverse effects when mixed with other medications. They also will not know if you desire to be kept on life support indefinitely or if you prefer to subscribe to the standard "right-to-die" language that is typically found in an advanced healthcare directive. The standard "right-to-die" language expresses your desire to not have your life unreasonably prolonged. If the medical team is unaware of your wishes, they aren't able to honor those wishes.

Having a California Advanced Healthcare Directive allows you to have your wishes honored through standardized legal documentation that is widely accepted in medical facilities. Without this, your family members may have their hands tied when it comes to your medical care and may be forced to seek court approval to make medical decisions on your behalf.

Benjamin Franklin said, "An ounce of prevention is worth a pound of cure." We consider this healthcare document to be your ounce of prevention. It's one way of taking a proactive approach for life's unexpected tragedies.

A Durable Financial Power of Attorney

Similar to the Advance Healthcare Directive, the Durable Financial Power of Attorney (POA) allows one to appoint a trusted individual to make critical financial decisions upon incapacity, and in some instances, without incapacity if the grantor of the power so chooses. The power granted in this legal document can be very broad or limited to a few financial responsibilities. It really depends on the language of the document. For instance, you may want to give your agent the power to access your bank account for the purpose of paying your mortgage and car payment, but prohibit them from selling your home.

Including a POA as part of your comprehensive estate planning may save your household from financial ruin if you are incapacitated for an extended period of time. Moreover, it may help to preserve your good credit by allowing your agent the power to pay creditors on your behalf.

As it pertains to married couples, there is an erroneous belief that a spouse automatically has power of attorney over the incapacitated spouse's property. This is not the case as many spouses have separate property in their names alone such as real estate, bank accounts, investment accounts, retirement plans, and other assets. A financial institution will not allow a spouse to access and control this property without the express written consent of the incapacitated spouse who owns the account or property. *The key here is the spouse's separate property or accounts only bearing the name of the incapacitated spouse. This may not be an issue for jointly held accounts.* Nonetheless, this properly conveys this power to a spouse or a trusted individual who may wisely manage your resources until your health condition has improved.

Nonetheless, despite the POA's importance in your plan, it is not without limitations. The most significant limitation often lies with the internal policies of a particular financial institution, which may choose to accept or reject the POA that you've prepared. Here's a pro tip: Once your POA has been prepared by your attorney, have it reviewed by the financial institution where it shall be used to ensure that it meets their internal policies.

Final Disposition Instructions

Finally, your estate plan is not complete without the written expression of your wishes as it pertains to your remains once you have passed away. As we like to say here at Legacy One Law Firm, "Your body, your choices, honored." At the most fundamental level, there is burial or cremation of your remains. At a more detailed and elaborate level, there are ashes planted in various urns and other exotic arrangements that appeal to the unique tastes and interests of the testator. For instance, we recently had a client request to be cremated and have their ashes interred in an apple tree urn, while another requested to have their ashes scattered at a specific set of GPS coordinates on a map.

Regardless if you are one to keep it simple or would prefer a detailed final ceremony, your Final Disposition Instructions should include the following: whether you prefer burial or cremation, the contact information of any funeral home where you have a contract for pre-made arrangements such as a gravesite and headstone, instructions for the distribution of your ashes if cremated, and the names of the primary and reserve agents who will oversee this process.

A failure to communicate your wishes in writing could result in family disputes due to mixed messages regarding your final wishes and differing opinions among family members. Remember: just because it may not matter to you, doesn't mean that it will not matter to those you leave behind.

CHAPTER 4

ESTATE PLANNING FOR CHILDREN

If you are a parent of minor children living in the home, you should take the step to have both temporary and long-term guardianship nominations. In many families and cultures, having a godmother or godfather is typical. It's the general understanding that, should anything happen to the parents, the godparents will take care of the surviving children. In California and many other states, however, godparents aren't legally recognized and thus, they do not have any legal authority to care for children in the absence of the natural parents. They, too, must petition the court through the formal guardianship process.

What the court will recognize after the death of both parents is a notarized or witnessed guardianship nomination that was created by either parent having natural parental rights.

When selecting a suitable guardian for a child, whether the parents are married or single does play a part in the planning process. For married couples, in an ideal scenario, both parents will agree upon the person(s) being named as temporary and/or long-term guardians of their children. It should be noted that under the law each spouse has parental rights. Therefore, each shall make separate nominations which may or may not match. In the event that one parent should die, the other parent has custody rights. However, if the surviving parent dies later, the nomination of that surviving parent will likely stand should they also pass away; provided however, the surviving spouse did not remarry and the child was adopted by the step-parent. For single parents, the process is not much different from a legal standpoint provided there is a willing and able natural parent who will claim custody of the child after the death of the other parent. If legal custody had been awarded to the deceased parent, there will certainly be court involvement before the surviving natural parent will be recognized as the lawful parent.

Temporary Guardians

Appointing temporary guardians is an essential element in keeping your children out of the custody and care of strangers in the event of death or incapacity. This person is a "first responder" in the event of an emergency where both parents cannot care for the child. In many cases, a great candidate for this role is the same person who has been named as the child's emergency contact upon registering them for school. The person you select as temporary guardian should be someone who is in close proximity to you and your family; one who your child already knows, trusts, and has a relationship with; and someone with whom your child is comfortable. Preferably, it should be the first person you would want to take custody and care for your child if you and your significant other were seriously injured in an accident.

Long-term Guardians

A long-term guardian is the person who is going to step into your shoes and raise your child to adulthood in the event that you and your significant other are unable to do so. This nomination should be given substantially more thought given the impact that it will likely have on your child over an extended period of time. Perhaps the most appropriate candidate is a close family member, such as a sibling or parent with whom you share similar values. Alternatively, it may be the godparent or the same person who you've nominated as the temporary guardian.

At any rate, when determining your long-term guardianship nomination, keep in mind that you are casting your vote for the most suitable candidate to raise your child, so there are some important things to consider. Below is a list of several factors to be mindful of before making your selection:

- Do they share your values?

You don't want your child to be raised by someone who doesn't share similar values to your own. It's important to ensure that the long-term guardian shares in your religious, social, educational and moral values.

- Family dynamics: Will it be a single or two-parent household with other children present?

Many parents may be particular about whether or not their child or children are raised in a two-parent household for any number of reasons. If this is important to you, it should certainly be considered when naming a long-term guardian. Raising a child can be physically and emotionally challenging for households with two active parents. Consider whether your child may be disadvantaged financially or likely to receive sufficient attention from the prospective guardian(s). Moreover, the presence of other children in the guardians' home will certainly have an impact on your child's experience. For instance, whether the guardians have experience raising children of their own or whether or not your child gets along well with the children of that household.

- What is the proximity of the guardian?

Proximity is key if you want your children to remain in the same school district or in the same state where they are currently residing. Are you comfortable with the idea of your child being relocated to another state or another country in the event of your death?

Perhaps you are thinking that the chances of both you and your spouse meeting an untimely death simultaneously are slim. Though that may be true, mathematically speaking, consider what would happen if tragedy were to strike and both you and your spouse are killed in a car accident. For single parents, you may be all that your child has. In either case, what would happen to your children?

In most parts of the country, standard protocol after a fatality will likely proceed according to these guidelines: The law enforcement officials are going to check your identification at the scene of the accident or at the emergency room. They may not be certain whether or not you have children, but they may seek clues at the scene such as the presence of a child seat in the back of your vehicle. At any rate, they must notify the next of kin or other family members. Thus, upon arriving at your house to find a babysitter with your children, if that individual doesn't have legal documentation authorizing *them* to take short-term custody of your children, your children may wind up in the custody and care of child protective services, or a similar agency designated for minor children who are similarly situated. So, in addition to the emotional trauma of losing their parents, your children may be removed from the home and thereby subjected to further discomfort.

As discussed in the previous chapter, you are in the best position to determine who will step into your shoes in the event of a short-term or permanent absence as a parent. The court only has limited or cursory knowledge of anyone stepping forward to petition for custody of your child. It is our belief at Legacy One Law Firm that the welfare of your family members (especially minor children) should be considered first, before considerations about assets are made. As a parent writing this book, and one who has experienced the paralyzing fear of an auto accident, I cannot stress the importance of finalizing this step as part of your comprehensive estate plan.

No One-Size-Fits-All Estate Plans

We understand that estate planning can feel overwhelming when you aren't sure where to start or what to include. There is no cookie-cutter approach to estate planning, unfortunately. Each family has their own unique set of family dynamics that makes their family their own. Working together with an experienced estate planning lawyer can alleviate many of your uncertainties and ensure that your specific family dynamics are all taken into account to create the most comprehensive estate plan that's right for you and your loved ones. Below are some common issues that we encounter while planning with families who have children.

Special Needs Children

You may have a special needs child with autism or some other type of disability that prevents them from being fully autonomous. Perhaps they receive state or federal benefits due to their existing condition. If this applies to you, please understand that an inheritance that you leave to them may disqualify them from further receiving state or federal benefits, unless proper measures are taken in advance.

There is special trust planning that can be established to help ensure that your child is not disqualified from receiving benefits due to receiving an inheritance left by you. We encourage all families that have children with special needs and disabilities to have a conversation with a qualified attorney to discuss what type of special planning should be put in place for those children regardless of whether they are minors or adults.

Minor Or Adult Children Lacking Financial Maturity

As discussed previously, there are issues when you have minor as well as adult children who aren't yet financially responsible or prepared to receive an inheritance. We briefly discussed the college-age child's dilemma after receiving an inheritance. However, there are a number of other potential issues that arise when leaving life insurance policies, real estate, retirement accounts, and other assets to children under the age of 18. When these assets are left to them outright and unprotected, those assets could end up in the hands of less responsible parents or other legal guardians that may not have your child's best interest at heart.

Substance Abuse Concerns

There may be a valid concern regarding substance abuse for a child who has been named as a beneficiary of a trust or left property via a will. The danger is clear: an unstable child or adult may have access to hundreds or thousands of dollars, if not more.

Having that kind of money coupled with substance abuse issues greatly increases the odds of this person inflicting harm upon themselves or others. Be sure to discuss with your estate attorney the relevant provisions that can be drafted to safeguard the health of your child or adult beneficiary. Doing so may save the life of a loved one and preserve assets that might have taken a lifetime to acquire.

Business Owner Parents

For parents who are business owners, you must consider what you desire to happen to your business in the event of your death or incapacity. If you want your business to pass on to your children, are your children ready to inherit that business? If they aren't at an age where they're mature enough to assume the responsibility of running a business, a formal business succession plan may be put in place. Business assets are part of one's personal estate at death. In Chapter 7, we will discuss what happens to one's business at death in greater detail. However, for the purpose of this chapter, if your child is to be included as part of your business' legacy, having provisions that address the transfer of your business to your child cannot be overlooked.

To conclude, there are many considerations to explore while doing estate planning with minor or young-adult children. Your plans will be largely dictated by your individual family dynamics, the personalities and abilities of your children, and several other factors that may not be covered in this book. Your children, regardless of age, are the very essence of your family legacy. Some of us would have never given thought to prudent estate planning had it not been for the sake of our children. I encourage you to take action today, and help make life a bit easier for them, in the event of your absence. Their future depends on it.

CHAPTER 5

ESTATE PLANNING FOR A LIFETIME

I recall the look of relief on her face as the shackles of fear, which gripped her mind, had been broken. Her eyes glimmered brighter and her smile sprang forth with less effort. Mrs. "B", a widow in her late 70's who had just finalized her estate plan after decades of procrastinating, could now breathe easier. She told me that she had waited so long to put a plan in place because *she was afraid that once she did, she*

would then pass away. As I write this book, years after drafting her living trust and other essential documents, Mrs. B is still alive and well. To her, estate planning was planning for death, and she was certainly not alone in this rather grim sentiment toward life and legacy planning.

Perhaps one of the greatest misconceptions about estate planning is the belief that it is a one-time transaction, which includes several legal documents that are focused on death. Once completed, the documents are to be placed in a binder that will never see the light of day, unless there is death or a tragic life event. Only then will a family member or close friend be compelled to dig through boxes and clutter to find one's woeful last wishes… And so on and so forth…

We get it! Estate planning is not now nor will it ever be the thrilling topic of discussion at the holiday party. In keeping with our belief that estate planning is planning for life, not death, this chapter will provide examples of when a holistic approach to planning that focuses more on life is beneficial to individual and family legacy.

Estate Planning to Protect Your Credit

If you become incapacitated, you will likely lose the ability to manage your financial affairs, and as a consequence, your financial health, including your credit rating may be negatively impacted. Many of us work hard to build what we consider a good credit score or rating. In an instant, this credit rating could be compromised or damaged should you be hospitalized for months and become delinquent on your mortgage or other financial obligations. A negative mark on your credit can last up to seven years or more depending on the type of account impacted.

With a carefully drafted durable financial power of attorney, you can ensure that a trusted family member or friend has access to your financial resources to pay bills on your behalf, if you lose the ability to do so on your own. A strong credit rating is something that can be leveraged over the course of a lifetime, and accordingly, key provisions in your legal documents should protect this aspect of your financial life. With that said, we recommend not settling for a standardized template version of power of attorney that oversimplifies or omits essential legal language. Many of these can be found online and they are not customized for your situation. Conversely, the POA documents that we prepare for clients often exceed 7-10 pages of legal language covering various financial circumstances that may impact our clients during incapacity. A downloadable form merely checking off boxes in many cases doesn't account for situations where the law requires specific authorization such as the management of real estate, retirement assets, government benefits, estate planning, and other nuanced financial matters. Therefore, if maintaining great credit and ensuring that your financial life remains intact are important, then I encourage you to include a durable financial power of attorney in your comprehensive estate plan.

Estate Planning in the Golden Years

Let's face it, this "old flesh" as some of the seniors in my community would often say, will eventually give out on us all. For some, the decline will come gradually, for others without a moment's notice. In Chapter 2, we discussed why it's never too soon to start planning. Unfortunately, there are times when it is too late. With that said, incapacitation is a part of many of our lives, whether it's in the form of diminished mental capacity or diminished physical capacity, whether it is you or a dear family member, its effects will certainly impact the family unit in some shape or form. A well-thought-out estate plan will speak to the phase of life where a natural decline in health can manifest in the form of diseases like Alzheimer's or dementia, which often result in the loss of the capacity to care for one's self in whole or in part. As it pertains to our topic, the loss of ability to plan for one's self is a cause for concern, and is an issue that we encounter when taking calls from concerned individuals seeking our services on behalf of another family member or close friend.

Unfortunately, when we reach the Golden Years, meaning the late years in life when one has grown old, we become more susceptible to losing the ability to manage and plan for our own financial affairs. This includes the ability to prepare a will, living trust, healthcare directives, and financial powers of attorney. The failure to get these essential documents in place *before* the loss of capacity occurs can result in several thousands of dollars in legal fees associated with obtaining a conservatorship, which is granted by the courts. A conservatorship is a court-appointed guardianship whereby one person is granted authority to manage the financial and/or personal affairs of another person. As mentioned earlier, anytime the court gets involved you will likely stay longer than you want to stay and pay more than you want to pay.

Effective planning also accounts for whether one desires to reside in a retirement home, Medicaid and Medi-Cal planning, as well as the considerations and costs involved with long-term care planning. It's prudent that one understands the intersection between estate planning and long-term care planning and discusses whether or not there will be an estate left after caring for one's self or a loved one.

To find out what long-term care will look like and all of the factors and considerations involved, speaking with an estate planning attorney and a licensed financial professional would be your next best step. They can address taking a proactive approach by getting in front of potential problems, as opposed to merely reacting to your demise at this phase of life. Based on what we've seen with the elderly members of our community, the former approach is vastly less costly than the latter.

DIY Estate Planning In The Digital Age

We see a much different issue facing the younger generations as it pertains to estate planning: The "DIY" or Do-It-Yourself approach. In today's digital age, with the advent of Artificial Intelligence (AI) and a host of other online platforms designed to place the power in the hands of consumers, what one doesn't know may certainly hurt them. If not the person using the DIY platforms to create a will or trust, then the children or other heirs of their estate in the future. One of the primary concerns with the DIY approach to estate planning is that it employs a cookie-cutter, one-size-fits-all methodology that hopes the end user will know which options or features to select in the software that's provided. It assumes that one knows the laws or the potential issues that might affect their household. Most often, it is merely a digital template that allows for very minimal customization, and as a result, it doesn't take into account the long-term goals or the nuances of *your* specific family dynamics. And, as we've discussed, this one-size-fits-all approach simply doesn't work in the grand scheme of planning for your legacy.

You might be thinking that my observation is self-serving because I would prefer that folks just hire attorneys. Well, although that may be partially true, based on the numerous living trusts that our firm has reviewed, which had been generated by low-cost DIY estate planning tools online, these documents neglect to address several of the following aspects:

- Whether you or your spouse have children from other marriages,
- Planning for children or adults with disabilities,
- Whether you have children or other beneficiaries with bad spending habits,
- Your particular values (i.e., religious, cultural, educational or familial)
- Succession of a business and its assets, and
- Family heirlooms or intellectual property that should be managed in a particular way.

Finally, arguably the most valuable component missing from the DIY approach is a relationship with a trusted advisor who will provide guidance and counsel long after the documents have been drafted and signed. A trusted advisor will help uncover the potential blind spots in your thinking because, quite frankly, you don't know what you don't know. Therefore, we recommend saving the DIY approach for your next home improvement project where at worst you can call a contractor to fix what's done incorrectly. Whereas, a misguided estate plan can impact your family legacy for years after your passing.

Estate Planning For Every Phase

Every milestone or phase of life could potentially require some level of attention in your estate plan. Some of the milestones that we help individuals and families consider may include, but are not limited to the following:

- Getting married
- Buying a home
- Having children
- Planning for college
- Retirement
- The birth of grandchildren

At each of these life stages, your assets, beneficiaries, and your wishes may be subject to change. As such, your living trust should be treated as a living document that evolves as your life evolves.

One of the primary ways that we see estate plans fail is that they're left unattended and outdated. Children are no longer minors, property has changed hands, laws have changed, etc. I must reiterate that estate planning is not a one-time or one-off event. It is something that should be revisited periodically to ensure that your wishes are still accurately articulated in writing.

To recap this chapter, we have discussed the various ways that an estate plan can add value to your life. Whether one is planning in the Golden Years of Life or early adulthood, a holistic approach that considers your short-term, intermediate, and long-term goals is essential. Under the advice and counsel of a trusted advisor, such as a qualified estate planning attorney, you can unlock the full potential of your estate plan over the course of your lifetime.

CHAPTER 6

ESTATE TAX: HOW IT WORKS

Estate taxes may be imposed against an individual's assets at the time of death. The Federal (and some state's) government has established laws that dictate how estate taxes work and whether a particular estate is subject to them based on the value or size of the estate at the death of the taxpayer.

Disclaimer: I am not a licensed tax professional nor is this chapter intended to serve as tax advice for the reader. Our goal here is to familiarize you with the Federal estate tax exemption, which establishes the basis for tax liability once its threshold has been exceeded.

As for state-level estate taxes, at the time of this book's publication, there are only 12 states that impose an estate tax upon one's passing. Fortunately, California, the state where our firm is licensed to practice, is not one of these states. If you are a reader residing in a different state, you may inquire online, consult a tax attorney, or ask your tax preparer whether your state imposes an estate tax. In short, here's how the federal estate tax exemption works: At the time of this publication (2024), the federal gift and estate tax exemption is $13.61 million per individual. However, for married couples, the exemption amount doubles ($27.22 million) and thereby provides for a larger accumulation of wealth that may not be subject to federal estate taxes. If the value of the estate at the time of death of the taxpayer exceeds the exemption amount, that estate is subject to tax rates of approximately 40%. Keep in mind that the rate of taxation and the exemption amount are subject to change and are based on the laws in effect at the time of the taxpayer's death. Again, consult with an attorney or tax professional to see what applies in your situation.

Some may read this chapter and think that this information is useful only to the rich, however, that may not be the case as the laws are subject to change. In fact, the federal estate tax exemption threshold is voted on by Congress periodically, and various political and economic factors are considered when setting the exemption threshold. For instance, the federal exemption was $2 million per person in 2007, and $5.4 million in 2015. If the projections that the exemption will drop by several millions in 2025 are accurate, we may see an exemption threshold of $5-7 million per individual. This will expose a significantly larger amount of the population to taxation at death by simply casting a wider net. For the purposes of this book, we will not delve into the reasoning behind these projections, but please be mindful of the existence of an exemption for estate taxation and consult with an estate attorney and tax professional for strategies to minimize liability for your estate. Some of the possibilities will be discussed below.

Advanced Planning Tools

There are three advanced planning tools that can be utilized to decrease the size of one's estate and thereby minimize tax liability at death. A brief overview of the various planning strategies includes:

1. Gifting Strategies

You may wish to avoid estate taxing by giving away some of your assets during your lifetime. For instance, the federal gift tax exclusion in 2023 was approximately $17,000 per individual recipient of such gift. This meant that during that tax year one could have given up to $17,000, or a total of $34,000 (if married), in gifts to children, grandchildren, or other individuals.

To clarify, this annual exclusion amount permitted one to give away up to $17,000 to as many people as desired without those gifts counting against the $12.9 million dollar lifetime gift tax exemption for 2023. Staying under this threshold eliminates the need to file a federal gift tax return. Therefore, gifting strategies are one way to reduce the overall size of one's estate prior to death, if the possibility of exceeding the exemption amount is an apparent threat. However, gifting strategies should only be employed under the advice of *your* attorney or a qualified tax professional.

2. Irrevocable Trust

As discussed in Chapter 3, while a revocable living trust may be altered, amended, changed, and discarded by the individual who creates it, an irrevocable trust generally cannot be changed or amended without court intervention and approval. One benefit of an irrevocable trust is that it can minimize the size of one's estate by removing those assets from the settlor's estate. Transferring property into an irrevocable trust with its own tax identification number constitutes a transfer to another entity, which is separate and distinct from the taxpayer. The taxpayer no longer owns the property, but has named beneficiaries who will in the future.

For example, if you put your $1 million home into an irrevocable trust, you have essentially reduced the size of your taxable estate by a million dollars. The home is no longer in your name, but deeded in the name of the trust, and that trust cannot be changed or amended by you. The settlor of the trust may name beneficiaries who may assume ownership of the property after the death of the settlor.

3. Irrevocable Life Insurance Trust (ILIT)

An irrevocable life insurance trust (ILIT) is a type of trust that is funded during your lifetime with one or more insurance policies. It's irrevocable, which means that once you create an ILIT, this trust can generally not be changed or revoked. It is subject to the terms that are outlined in the trust agreement. The use of an ILIT to hold life insurance could help you avoid having your policy's death benefit included in your taxable estate at death.

At the same time, you control how and when the death benefit is used and to whom it is given. It could also provide the cash needed to cover estate taxes or other expenses after you have passed away. Furthermore, it may assist in leveraging the annual gift tax exclusion by excluding those "gifts" in the form of insurance premiums, which are held by the trust.

These are just a few of the strategies that can be utilized to help minimize the overall size of your estate for tax planning purposes. As with any estate planning-related decision, it's important to check with a qualified estate attorney and tax professional to determine which strategy is best for you.

CHAPTER 7

PROTECTING YOUR BUSINESS AT DEATH

During the summer of 2021, I was approached by a friend and strategic business partner to write an article for *Business Matters Magazine* to address some of the pitfalls and considerations that business owners must face when planning for death and the succession of their businesses. Unfortunately, business assets are often overlooked as a part of estate planning. We often hear during consultations, "We want to make sure the kids get the house" only to find out several minutes later that they own a thriving business that's worth more than the family home. Naturally, when we're thinking about business, we're not thinking directly about family matters. We're likely thinking about generating revenue and building wealth that will support the family, and if approaching retirement, we may then give thought to passing the business down at some point in the future. There are, however, four key questions that you should consider *today* if you are a business owner, co-owner, or partner with significant interest in a business:

1. What if something happens to you (as in death or incapacity) as the business owner or one of the other business owners in the company?
2. Would your business sink or swim in your absence?
3. How would your loved ones receive your share of the corporation, LLC or other business interest?
4. How would the business be passed on or managed in your absence?

If you find yourself puzzled or clueless after asking those questions, and you and/or your business partners do not have a written strategy drafted by your legal team or other financial professionals, a business succession plan may be put in place.

There are several critical components to a comprehensive business succession plan that we will discuss in this chapter. Based on the four key questions above, the first thing to consider is whether you *should* have a business succession plan in place to begin with. A qualified business or estate planning attorney can help you determine this. Nevertheless, the bottom line is that your business assets are also a part of your personal estate. Thus, without a written plan in place, your corporation, LLC, general partnership or sole proprietorship could very easily end up in probate court along with your home and other personal assets. Please keep in mind that the aforementioned business entity types are not meant to be an exhaustive list of the business structures that are subject to probate. However, regardless of the type of formal or informal business structure you have in place, your death or incapacity could result in the destruction of your business without proper planning. Furthermore, not having adequate insurance in place can also wipe out your business in the event of your demise, even if your business partner(s) intend to carry on the business after your death.

As business owners, we have additional considerations to address to ensure the assets we've worked hard to acquire ultimately end up in the right hands. In this chapter, we'll discuss three tips that may help business owners pass down their estates, which consist of both personal and business assets, in a timely and cost-efficient manner.

Purchase Adequate Insurance

It's well-established that life insurance should be included in most business owners' asset portfolios. However, traditional life insurance is designed to provide *personal* financial resources to loved ones or other beneficiaries upon the insured's death. Conversely, "Key Person Insurance" (KPI) is a type of insurance policy that provides a monetary death benefit to a business if its owner or another essential employee passes away. KPI may be vital for businesses that may be adversely impacted by the death of the owner or "key" employee. Moreover, the cash infusion from KPI may be used to satisfy business debts, partnership buyouts, and other costs associated with a business owner's passing.

Again, I cannot overemphasize or overstate the importance of having adequate life insurance policies, particularly, key person insurance. Here's why: If you were to pass away tomorrow, and your business is valued at $5 million dollars, your share wouldn't go directly to your family, it would go to your estate. And what would happen if your business partner had to write a check for $2.5 million dollars to your estate? For most businesses, it would mean financial ruin without the proper KPI in place to provide financial support in the wake of the death of key personnel or key ownership interest in the business.

Business Succession Planning

Who will carry on the legacy of your business when you're gone? Business Succession Planning involves the proper planning, insurance, and legal agreements necessary to facilitate the efficient settlement of your estate at death. Additionally, it should facilitate a smooth succession or transition of power when something has happened to one of the business owners, either through death or incapacity. Whether you're a sole proprietor, in a partnership, or other type of business entity, having a documented strategy for what happens at your death or that of another partner is critical to minimizing legal disputes and other financial quarrels among stakeholders and family members. If the intent is to have your business thrive after your death, then a conversation with a qualified advisor regarding this type of planning is critical.

A business succession plan often includes buy-sell agreements that work in conjunction with operating agreements, bylaws of a corporation, life insurance policies that include key person insurance, and a comprehensive estate plan (Yes, a business succession plan should still be supported by and consistent with the provisions described in your own estate plan).

A buy-sell agreement is an agreement that you formalize in writing, stating what happens to your role and position when something happens to you. If you're the CEO of a company or a founding member of an LLC, you must put in writing what happens to your percentage and who is going to take over your role and responsibilities. An oral agreement may have no legal effect and leave many questions unanswered.

With that said, if you pass away or become incapacitated, will your business be wrapped up and sold? Will it continue under a different manager or leader? If so, who will the manager be? Who will make critical decisions for your business if something happens to you? Your business succession plan will include details that address all of these questions.

Estate Planning for Business Owners

What good is it to have buy-sell agreements and all of these life insurance policies to only have your business wind up in probate court? You guessed it: not much good at all. This is why having your own comprehensive estate plan in place is so essential. Moreover, encouraging your business partner(s) to have one in place might save you from the unnecessary hassle and expenses that arise from its absence.

In short, your business assets/interests could wind up in the costly and time-consuming probate process. Moreover, each year in the United States, billions of dollars in assets are categorized as "unclaimed property" by state government agencies. Business assets that have been unaccounted for by deceased business owners make up a significant portion of this staggering figure. A revocable living trust with appropriate provisions for your business assets may be the best instrument for avoiding court, conflict, and efficiently transferring your business assets. Even in instances where KPI and a Business Succession Plan have not been established, a comprehensive Estate Plan can mitigate the risk of loss. Seek the advice of a qualified attorney to discuss the planning needs of your business in more detail.

Undoubtedly, KPI, Business Succession Planning, and Estate Planning are essential to securing your business's legacy. You've worked diligently to build your empire, why not implement the appropriate planning to preserve it?

CHAPTER 8

THE COLLABORATION OF ESTATE, TAX, AND FINANCIAL PLANNING–YOUR "LEGACY DREAM TEAM"

As we continue on our journey of exploring the holistic approach to estate planning, we now reach the point of discussing the importance of your relationship with a team of trusted advisors who will help navigate the process of securing your legacy through wealth building, wealth preservation, and compliance with tax laws. I've dubbed this your "Legacy Dream Team."

Consider this: What good is it to spend a lifetime building assets only to have them squandered or taken away due to a lack of knowledge? In reality, you will likely only be good as the team that you build around you. This principle holds true in sports, business, friendships, and of course, legacy planning. To maximize your access to knowledge, which will facilitate prudent planning, these are the three professional advisors that should be present on your Legacy Dream Team:

- A qualified financial professional,
- A qualified tax professional, and
- A qualified estate planning attorney.

These three professionals should work together to ensure that your best interest is top priority at all times. Your financial, retirement, and investment planners will help you build wealth; your tax professional will help you lawfully retain much of your wealth, and finally, your estate planning attorney will develop the strategy to ensure wealth is preserved for generations to come. Now, for those readers who believe that they are not likely to leave behind a fortune (and that's most of us), the same team should be established to help manage what you do have.

It should be noted that it is vital that each member of your team stays in their respective lane and does not offer advice in areas where they have not obtained licensure or proper training. For example, a qualified and prudent estate planning attorney will take into consideration the financial planning that you've already put in place without encroaching or "stepping on the toes" of your financial advisor. Typically, financial planning, retirement planning, and investment planning include the management of various financial instruments that can be divided into asset classes. During the estate planning process, your attorney should discuss the what, the how, and the when as it pertains to the distribution of those assets to your beneficiaries. However, if there is a disagreement or conflict between professionals on how a particular asset should be distributed or managed in your living trust, then you, as the captain of your team, should arrange a team meeting to cordially address the matter and come to a resolution that best serves you, the client.

One example of how we might strategize with a client regarding a particular asset class is the use of life insurance proceeds to meet the long-term goals of distributing a particular asset that is held by the trust. There are several ways that we can use life insurance in your trust that may mitigate estate taxes, if applicable, or more commonly help pay off a mortgage on a home to be left to beneficiaries. For instance, many families desire to leave the family home to their kids free and clear of any mortgage. If adequate insurance is available, those proceeds may be used to pay off the remaining mortgage balance, so the children are not burdened with the responsibility of that debt while enjoying the home that you've left for them.

Finally, most estate planning attorneys are not also licensed tax professionals. As discussed in an earlier chapter, having a revocable living trust alone will not impact an individual's tax liability during one's lifetime. However, as it pertains to estate planning, there may be concerns about estate taxes and how one may employ various tax strategies to minimize tax at death. For those utilizing irrevocable trusts, which have their own federal tax identification numbers, the filing of annual tax returns on the income generated by that trust may be required. This is where having a relationship with a trusted tax professional is essential to lawfully securing your family legacy and maximizing what is available to your heirs via inheritance. Tax reduction strategies may be in your best interest as a prudent planner depending on your overall net worth.

Common Planning Pitfalls

Now that we've covered some of the advantages of developing a relationship with a qualified team of professionals, let's examine some of the pitfalls that may be encountered by those who attempt to do it alone or take the DIY approach to planning.

1. Planning with Only A Simple Will

One of the most common estate planning pitfalls that we see occur without expert guidance is relying on a traditional or simple will. As discussed earlier in this book, because of the long-standing tradition surrounding wills, it's easy to believe that a will is sufficient to keep your family out of court and conflict. We've now established this as a misconception. Having access to a qualified estate attorney will shed light on the inherent limitations to simply creating a will, without any other estate planning documents in your plan. Remember, the courts do not have the time or resources to preserve the wealth that you've left behind. They are merely there to make distributions according to what you have set forth in your will after paying the creditors with a rightful claim to a share of your estate. Unfortunately, the bills don't simply vanish at our passing.

With that in mind, in the absence of a trusted team of advisors, your personal knowledge of making distributions may be severely limited. For example, a prudent advisor would likely discover that you have minor children, and the law doesn't permit gifts to be given directly to them without court involvement and other restrictions in place. Under the Uniform Transfer Of Minors Act, or UTMA, these laws place restrictions on parents leaving gifts through a will directly to children under the age of 18.

There are several cases where a divorced or single parent passes away and leaves a life insurance policy and other assets as gifts to children via a simple will. Unfortunately, what those well-intentioned parents did not know is that someone else, usually the surviving parent or court-appointed guardian, may have access to those funds and property that were meant for the benefit of the child. After the court made the distribution to the child or to their guardians on their behalf, the inheritance was unprotected and ended up in the wrong hands or mismanaged. Conversely, if those assets were properly planned for under the guidance of professional advisors, the assets left for those children might have been protected and preserved through the provisions of a living trust.

2. Naming The Wrong Beneficiaries

All too often, we see people naming other people as beneficiaries on life insurance policies and bank accounts, as well as individual retirement accounts. Some erroneously believe that this step constitutes a well thought out plan for the intended beneficiary. After all, they will be receiving a check, right? Although they mean well, this is problematic because they are most likely naming loved ones who are very close, and unfortunately, those individuals are more likely to pass away together in the event of a serious accident. Moreover, if the beneficiaries named on all of your policies and accounts have passed away with you, those assets are vulnerable to being lost to the state because there's no surviving beneficiary nor is there a contingent plan in place to address this type of tragedy. Finally, naming your minor child as a beneficiary, as discussed earlier, comes with a host of other issues from squandering to outright theft by those who don't have your child's best interest at heart. Your estate attorney, as a vital member of your Legacy Dream Team, can provide solutions to ensure the proper beneficiary designations are made and these assets are not lost or end up in the hands of an unintended beneficiary.

3. Joint Ownership Of Property

The final misguided approach to planning is simply adding a child or beneficiary to the title of a property while the parent is still alive. This is often seen in real estate transactions where a parent wishes to give their house to their children without going through the proper estate planning process. Although this may appear to be the convenient and low-cost option, it is not a prudent method of passing down the home. In short, there are several tax and legal ramifications for putting someone on the deed of your property while you are still alive.

Here are some things to consider before adding a child's or relative's name to the deed of your house:

1. Do you mind your child being a legal owner of the house immediately?
2. Do you mind your child being your new landlord and you having the obligation to pay your child rent in certain situations?
3. How do you feel about needing your child's permission to sell your property, if needed?
4. What happens with property taxes and other types of taxes?

Here, your estate planning attorney and tax professional can offer insight into how this course of action might affect all of the issues mentioned above.

To conclude, there are simply no shortcuts to having a comprehensive estate plan in place under the guidance of a team of professionals having experience in dealing with these matters. Avoiding these pitfalls, and others not mentioned in this book, can save your family or your heirs thousands in taxes and legal fees, not to mention the time it will take to unravel the issues in the long run. As a call to action, take the first step in assembling your Legacy Dream Team by either asking for a referral from an existing professional in your life or actively seeking the first member of your team by reading the online client reviews before scheduling a consultation to determine whether a particular individual or organization is a good fit.

CHAPTER 9

FINDING THE RIGHT ESTATE PLANNING ATTORNEY

We live in the information age, where it's all too common to have "Do-it-Yourself" anything. We can learn how to remodel our kitchens or perhaps take a course on gardening, all from the palm of our hands with our mobile devices. Furthermore, with the rise of Artificial Intelligence, we'll soon be able to ask our devices to produce complex literary works by harnessing the abundance of resources available online. However, before you drop this book and pick up the computer mouse, I urge you to consider hiring a qualified estate planning attorney to do the heavy lifting on your behalf.

The Internet and social media are full of lists. Top 5 of this, Top 10 of that… So here are my Top 3 reasons why finding the right estate planning attorney to help navigate this journey is the best option for you, your family, and your legacy.

 # 1… The Cost of Mistakes Outweighs the Benefits Of Doing it Yourself

The ramifications for making a mistake in this area are far too impactful and potentially life-altering to risk relying on software or technology that is designed to profit from the masses as opposed to ensuring what you care about is taken care of. Allow me to explain. On many occasions, we receive phone calls from beneficiaries wondering why they are still required to go to probate despite having a trust. They soon learn that this was due to not properly funding the trust and aligning the assets in a manner that would avoid probate completely. The creators of the trust were either misinformed or uninformed regarding critical steps in the process. As a result, the beneficiaries will incur substantial legal fees to fix what could have been done correctly the first time. As it pertains to life-altering impact, suppose your home ends up in probate as opposed to being strategically passed down in a properly funded trust, and the court fees and taxes associated with this process make it infeasible for your family to keep the home. Suddenly, the initial cost savings of using a website or document preparation service turn into a catastrophic loss. Therefore, what you don't know on the front end can cost your family dearly after your death or incapacity.

#2...Your Legacy is Much More than Documents and Forms

It's quite simple, the online technology supporting low-cost DIY estate planning options are nothing more than standardized templates, which don't account for your unique family dynamics. When it comes to life and legacy planning, customization is paramount. Only you know the family values, traditions, issues, spending habits, disabilities, strengths, and weaknesses of your immediate household. Moreover, let us not forget the issues involving extended family members that may impact your loved ones and assets in your absence. Therefore, simply filling out an online questionnaire that somehow drafts a trust that will accurately secure your family legacy and account for your personalized wishes is highly unlikely.

As a Reminder: The standardized online platforms often fail to take into account the needs of blended families, sibling relationships, special needs dependents, long-term care needs, college planning, or business succession planning. What milestone events in your child's life might you want to provide for in the event of your absence? How important are the people, the property, and the accomplishments that define your legacy? The value that you place on estate planning should reflect this.

#3...The Value of a Relationship Outweighs the Upfront Cost

Perhaps the greatest value that a trusted advisor can offer to a client is their availability in times of need. The right estate planning attorney will have systems and processes in place to continue the relationship with you far beyond drafting a will or a living trust. As I mentioned before, prudent estate planning is not a one-and-done, set-it-and-forget-it transaction. This is why you always get what you pay for when it comes to this type of planning. Having a mindset of planning for life means there will likely be circumstances where your relationship with your attorney will be vital. Whether it's a change in the laws, your assets, your beneficiaries, or your personal wishes, having someone in your corner who you know, like, and trust will pay dividends when faced with life's uncertainties.

Legacy One Law Firm: Let Us Give You Peace Of Mind

As we conclude this final chapter, there are four unique factors that make Legacy One Law Firm the preferred option for most Californians looking to embark upon estate planning: A holistic approach to estate planning, price transparency, an ongoing relationship, and planning beyond the drafting of legal documents.

A Holistic Approach To Estate Planning

Our approach takes into account your unique family dynamics, values, and long-term aspirations as opposed to the transactional document preparation approach that leaves many families in the dark when something happens to a loved one.

We Believe In Price Transparency

Several firms in California charge $400 to $500 per hour - and this can be very cost-prohibitive for many average, hard-working families. We don't subscribe to charging billable hours here, as we feel that system is outdated and intimidating for this type of service.

When you plan with us, you're not going to get a mysterious bill in the mail because we simply read an email or answered your phone call when a problem arose. We have transparent pricing that takes the guesswork out of getting this essential planning into place.

Our goal is to make ourselves available to you throughout your lifetime. This includes being considerate of your finances. Therefore, we charge a flat fee for the planning services that we provide. Knowing the price up front means no surprises - only the pleasant ones.

We're Here To Create An Ongoing Relationship

When life hits hard and when tragedy strikes home, who can you call? Many people who have estate plans prepared don't fully understand what the documents mean. They have a very cursory or fundamental education of how things work. As a result, they will likely hire another attorney just to figure out or interpret what they put in place the first time.

Education and empowerment are ingrained in our mission toward serving our clients. Not only will you understand the what and the why behind the plan that you've put in place, but you'll have the support of a trusted advisor as you encounter changes over the course of your lifetime. Perhaps the greatest value that we provide to you is our availability.

Planning Beyond the Draft

One of the most common ways that we see an estate plan fail is that it becomes outdated. It may sit on a bookshelf, untouched until tragedy strikes. To remedy that, we offer periodic reviews for all of our clients. Once you become a Legacy One Law client, you're entitled to have your estate plan reviewed every few years.

We'll help you tackle the potential issues when life changes, when your assets change, when the law changes, and when your wishes change. This means that you don't have to hope that your estate plan will carry over into every season of your life – you can be confident that it will.

What Is The Next Step?

Congratulations on completing this book. I hope that you were well informed and are now empowered to become the prudent planner that your family, business, or personal legacy needs. I'd like to personally thank you for your time and invite you to connect with me and my team directly to learn more about how we serve our clients and community.

If you would like to schedule a time to discuss starting your personal estate or business succession plan, please contact us here:

Via the web: www.legacyonelaw.com

Email: info@legacyonelaw.com

Phone: (323) 405-7017

What to expect during the process?

It all begins with an initial phone consultation or discovery call to learn more about your wishes. We then take a deeper dive with a live virtual or in-person planning session to explore what would happen right now if something happens to you based on the plan that you currently have in place. Then, if you decide to move forward, we will take 3-4 weeks to design an estate plan according to your unique family dynamics and wishes.

This simple and efficient process is designed to keep your family out of court and conflict, which may in turn save your family thousands in legal fees, ensure they are properly provided for, and help ensure those relationships are not damaged by the impact of your affairs not being in order.

Your loved ones will be grateful for the time you've invested with them in mind, and they will likely follow your example by doing the same for their future families, which, at its core, is the essence of securing generational wealth and prudent legacy planning.

INDEX

NOTES

Made in the USA
Monee, IL
03 November 2026

67385035R00075